The Minstrel
in the Tower

By Gloria Skurzynski

Illustrated by Julek Heller

A STEPPING STONE BOOK

Random House 🏠 New York

*For James Joseph Alm, a singer,
and his sister Stephanie, who climbs*

Library of Congress Cataloging-in-Publication Data:
Skurzynski, Gloria. The minstrel in the tower / by Gloria Skurzynski ; illustrated
by Julek Heller. p. cm.—(A Stepping stone book) SUMMARY: In the year 1195, eleven-
year-old Roger and his eight-year-old sister Alice must travel the French countryside
in search of their ailing mother's estranged brother, a wealthy baron. ISBN:
0-394-89598-3 (pbk.); 0-394-99598-8 (lib. bdg.) [1. Brothers and sisters—Fiction.
2. France—History—Medieval period, 987–1515—Fiction. 3. Middle Ages—
Fiction.] I. Heller, Julek, ill. II. Title. PZ7.S6287Mi 1988 [Fic]—dc19 87-26614

Manufactured in the United States of America   1   2   3   4   5   6   7   8   9   0

Contents

I. The Cottage

Alice heard the sweet singing of a nightingale. It sounded so perfect that a real nightingale might have been fooled, but not Alice. Her brother, Roger, had whistled the bird's song. It was their secret signal.

"I'm up here," she called.

"Are you in that tree again?" he cried, seeing Alice in the top branches of a huge sycamore. "You know you're not supposed to climb that high! Get down, you monkey."

"It's nice up here," Alice answered. "I can see so far! When Father returns from the Crusade, I'll be the first to see him coming."

Roger leaned against the trunk of the big old tree. "If he's ever going to come home at all," he said, "this would be a good time for it, with Mother so sick." It was the year 1195, and the Crusade had ended three years earlier. Mother, Roger, and Alice waited alone in their cottage, with only their elderly neighbor, Zara, to visit them. Since their mother had become ill, old Zara helped care for her.

"You'd better come down right now," Roger called, "before Zara starts looking for us. It scares her when she sees you up so high." Under his breath he added, "It scares me, too."

Roger was eleven; Alice was only eight. He tried to watch out for her the best he could, but Alice was hard to keep up with. She never walked when she could run, and she never stayed on the ground when she could climb.

"Children!"

"What did I tell you," Roger said as they heard old Zara shouting for them.

"Children! Where are you? Roger, is Alice with you? Alice, answer me!"

"Don't let her know I'm up here," Alice begged.

Roger was not only good at bird calls; he could imitate people's voices perfectly. In a voice that sounded exactly like Alice's, he called, "I'm here with Roger, Zara. At the big tree."

"Both of you come inside at once!" old Zara cried sharply.

"Something must be wrong!" Roger said. "Hurry, Alice!"

She scrambled down the tree so fast that he couldn't stand to watch. He turned away until he felt her next to him on the ground. Together they raced to the tiny cottage.

When they reached the door, they stopped in dismay. Their mother had risen from her sickbed to sit in the center of the room. Her long yellow hair spread from her head to her waist like rays of sunlight. In her lap rested a lute. As she bent forward to pluck its strings, she sang:

"My brother is a noble knight,
An eagle guards his shield of white,
My brother won't forgive a wrong,
His sword is steel, his arm is strong. . . ."

Old Zara stood wringing her hands. "I tried to make her stay in bed, but she won't listen. She's burning with fever."

"Mother!" Roger cried, running to her. "Go back and lie down!"

Spots red as strawberries stained their mother's cheeks, but her forehead and lips looked pale as winter. "Dear Roger," she said,

"let me sit while I can. Soon enough I'll lie forever, in my grave."

Fear sent prickles over Roger's skin. Alice looked frightened too. "Is Mother going to die?" she asked Zara.

"There, there, child," soothed the old woman. "When people get feverish, they say foolish things. You mustn't worry."

As their mother stared at Roger and Alice, she seemed to come to her senses. "I've been dreaming," she said, "about my brother, Raimond, in Bordeaux. It was such a real dream, I felt I could reach out and touch him."

"What brother?" Roger asked. "You don't have a brother."

"The truth is, I do have one, and you must find him, Roger. Tell Raimond I beg his forgiveness, and that I leave you children in his care. Who else will look after you when I'm gone? Your father must be dead, or he would have come back to us long ago."

Dead! Roger's fear turned to cold pain. He'd suspected Father might have died in battle, because most men had long since returned from the Crusade. To hear his mother say it, though, cut through to his heart. Maybe he didn't have to believe her. Maybe old Zara was right—that feverish people said foolish things.

Their mother had begun to pluck the lute again. With a sudden motion, she held out the instrument to Alice.

"Take this to your uncle Raimond," she told the girl. "Show him the eagle carved on the back. Ask him to come quickly. Quickly!" Her eyes grew wild, and then she fell into a faint.

"Catch her!" Zara cried.

"I don't want her to die," sobbed Alice as they carried their mother to the bed. Alice had no memory of her father, but her mother had always been there to hold her, to love and comfort her.

"All morning she's been talking about this brother, Raimond," Zara told them. "It's preying on her mind. I think she won't get well until you bring him to her."

"I don't even know where Bordeaux is," Roger protested.

"Three days east of here," Zara answered. She wrung her hands. "So far away!"

Alice was kneeling beside the bed. "Three whole days!" she exclaimed through her tears. "What will we eat?"

"You won't be going with me," Roger said.

"Yes I will!" She jumped to her feet. "Mother told me to. I'm supposed to take the lute to our uncle."

Roger could have argued that their mother's mind wasn't clear when she spoke those words. Yet in spite of himself he wanted Alice with him on the journey. All their lives they'd depended on each other for company. "All right," he answered. "But if you come, you have to obey me. As for food . . ." He pointed to the lute. "That will buy our suppers."

"No, I won't let you sell it!" Alice wrapped her arms around the pear-shaped lute. "Mother said—"

"I know what Mother said. I'm not going to sell it. I'm going to play it. Mother taught me all her songs. I'll sing for our suppers, like a strolling minstrel."

"I wish I could go in your stead," lamented Zara. "But I'm far too old to make such a journey." Her face puckered as she lifted the edge of her brown wimple to dab her eyes. "Don't worry about your mother— I'll tend her carefully while you're gone. It's you children I worry about! May heaven protect the two of you!"

II. The Journey

The sun hung halfway between straight-up noon and sunset. Since they'd started out from home Alice had been skipping ahead and running back, but now her steps lagged to match Roger's.

"I'm hungry," she told him.

Hunger didn't bother Roger so much, but other things did. With each step the lute bumped him. Because they were heading west, the sun shone right into his eyes. Long before, the road had turned away from the river Dordogne, and since then they hadn't found even a tiny brook they could drink from.

"You said you'd sing and play for our supper," Alice told him. "But we haven't seen a single traveler. So how are we going to eat?"

Right at that moment Roger noticed dust rising on the road ahead. "Someone's coming," he answered as though he'd expected it all along.

"I hope they have food and water with them, and I hope they like lute music," said Alice.

The sun stood bright behind the travelers so that when they reached the top of a small hill, they cast long shadows. They wore dark, ankle-length hooded gowns and carried the round-headed staffs of pilgrims. Pilgrims walked the roads all over Europe to pray at a single saint's shrine or at a number of shrines and churches. Roger saw that the two coming toward them were women. One was old, the other barely past her girlhood.

"Peace to you," Roger greeted them, and both women echoed, "Peace." Alice stayed silent, too awed by the beauty of the young girl to manage a greeting.

"I'm a strolling minstrel," Roger announced. "If you will share your supper with us, I'll sing a song for you."

The older woman frowned, staring down her nose at them. Roger knew that he and his sister looked like tatterdemalions. Their shabby clothes were covered with the dust of the road. Roger's wrists stuck out from his sleeves, and Alice's dress was patched in three places. For more than a year Mother hadn't made new clothes for either of them because she couldn't afford to buy cloth.

Annoyed at the woman's haughty look, Alice exclaimed, "My brother, Roger, is a wonderful singer! He knows all Mother's songs. He can imitate voices and bird calls too."

"Oh, Mama, let's share our food with these children," the lovely girl begged. "They look hungry, and we have enough for all."

"Humpf! I suppose so, Aurore," the mother answered with ill grace. Pursing her lips, she opened a leather pouch to take out bread and cheese and salted meat.

Since Alice didn't want to stare greedily, she pretended to watch a nightingale in a tree

nearby. Then she cried, "Look! Someone for-
got to pick the apricots in those top branches."
In a flash she'd tucked the hem of her skirt
into her belt and was climbing the tree.

"Be careful!" Aurore cried. "You might
fall!"

"You don't have to worry about Alice,"
Roger told her. "She's always climbing
something or other at home—trees or walls
or even the roof when it needs new thatch.
Our mother calls her *La Guenuche*—the
monkey in skirts."

Roger would rather have starved than
climb the apricot tree. Heights frightened
him, but Alice balanced easily in the top
branches. She flung the ripe fruit to Roger
until the tree was picked bare.

"Come down now, *La Guenuche,*" Aurore
called, laughing. "You've surely earned your
share of supper. Hasn't she, Mama?"

"Humpf!" the older woman snorted, already eating. Her manners were quite ele-
gant. She lifted dainty bits of meat to her
lips on the point of a knife, and she spit each
apricot pit into her hand before dropping it
to the ground.

"We're on a pilgrimage to the shrine at Rocamadour," Aurore told them. "We've already traveled a week." As she spoke the young girl lowered her hood.

Alice gasped at the beauty of Aurore's hair. It was the color of the apricots. Thick, wavy, and shining, it had been woven into one long braid that hung over her shoulder. The older woman noticed Alice's admiration and said, "Aurore will sacrifice her hair at Rocamadour. She's offering it so that her father may be cured of an illness."

"You mean, cut off her hair?" Roger asked, appalled.

"How else can she offer it, except to cut it off?" sniffed the woman, dabbing her lips.

Roger felt deeply sorry for poor Aurore, who looked sad at the mention of her coming sacrifice. Alice, though, touched her own dark, tangled curls and thought how nice it would be to have short hair that never needed combing to get the snarls out.

The woman stuffed each leftover crust back into the pouch. "We shall save these crumbs for any other beggars we meet on the way," she announced. "Now you may sing for us, minstrel."

Roger had no wish to perform for such a wretched woman, but he'd promised to sing for his supper. Turning toward Aurore, he plucked the strings of his lute and began:

> *"A singer and a strummer,*
> *Sweet are the tunes I play*
> *For you to greet the summer*
> *And dance the night away.*
> *Let old folks drowse and slumber,*
> *Youth loves a holiday."*

Then, on the spot, he made up a brand-new verse:

> *"The time will go by quickly,*
> *I promise you, Aurore,*
> *Your curls will grow back thickly,*
> *E'er summer comes twice more."*

Aurore's sad look disappeared. "You're right, of course, minstrel," she said with a smile. "Shorn hair does grow back."

"We must leave now," the mother fussed. "Come along, Aurore."

Until they were out of sight, Aurore kept turning around to wave and shout, "Farewell, minstrel! Thank you for the song! Farewell, *La Guenuche*!"

III. The Fork in the Road

"Which way do we go?" Alice asked.

Roger hadn't been paying attention, but Alice, as usual, had run ahead. She stood where the road forked, one part going left and the other right.

"I don't know," Roger said. There was nothing to show which direction led to Bordeaux.

"We can't go both ways," Alice declared. She picked a daisy from the side of the road and began to pluck its petals one by one. "Left path, right path," she said as she pulled each petal. "Left, right, left . . ." The last petal was a "right."

"We're not going to make up our minds because of a daisy. That's silly," Roger said. "We'll go left."

"It's just as silly to choose left because the daisy said right," Alice argued.

Roger was tired and worried, and there was no way to tell which road really led to Bordeaux. One direction was as good as the other. "You promised to obey me, and I pick left," he insisted.

"Oh, all right!"

An hour later the road had narrowed to the width of a lane. Trees grew so thickly on both sides that the branches met overhead. Around a bend, a fallen log blocked the path entirely.

"You should have listened to the daisy," Alice told him.

"We'll have to go back to the crossroads," Roger confessed. He wished there were someone to blame besides himself. "It's almost dark now, so we can't go back till morning."

"Where will we sleep?" Alice asked.

"This road—or what's left of it—must lead somewhere. We'll climb over the log and keep going till it's too dark to see."

As the trees grew more dense and the night deepened, the forest seemed to speak. Crickets chirred, leaves rustled, small animals chittered, and an owl asked *who* dared intrude into his domain. Ahead of him Roger could hear his sister breaking through brush. Then all was silent.

"Alice!" he called sharply. "Where are you?"

"Just ahead. Keep coming. I've found something."

"What is it? Answer me!" Darkness dropped over the forest like a lid on a chest.

"You'll see when you get here," she called.

Roger blundered through the trees in the direction of her voice. Suddenly something small and warm grabbed his arm. He nearly yelled, but it was only his sister's hand.

"Over there—see the round thing that looks darker than the shadows?" she asked. "It's a tower. We can sleep inside it tonight."

"No we won't! Snakes and spiders nest in dark places, and I need to take care of you. We'll sleep in the open."

"That's even better," Alice said. "The night's warm enough, and I don't have to worry about getting my dress dirty on the ground. It's already dirty."

"At least it still fits you. You never seem to get bigger, the way I do."

"Wouldn't it be nice if our uncle Raimond turned out to be rich and would buy us new clothes?" Alice asked, gathering leaves for a bed.

"He could turn out to be poor. Or he could turn out not to be real," Roger said. "Maybe he's just a dream from Mother's fever."

Alice didn't answer, and Roger realized she was crying. *I shouldn't have mentioned Mother,* he thought, feeling sorry and clumsy. "Don't cry," he told her. "I didn't mean what I said. I'm sure there's an uncle Raimond. We'll find him. Go to sleep now."

Roger sat against a tree and held the lute across his knees. He strummed it softly, hoping the music would soothe Alice so that she could sleep without sad dreams. The tune he strummed was a Crusader song that reminded him of his father.

Trumpets had blared, visors had flashed, and sword hilts had gleamed under the bright sky the day his father went away. Banners and shields bore coats of arms showing lions, griffins, falcons, or stars. Each man's right sleeve wore the cross of a Crusader.

Father had told Roger that the Crusade would be led by two kings: Philip of France and Richard the Lion-Hearted, who ruled the land of Aquitaine where they lived.

When dozens of noblemen rode past, mounted proudly on their war-horses, Roger had cheered and clutched his father's hand. Archers followed, some carrying crossbows, others bearing longbows. Then came hundreds of foot soldiers, with banners fluttering from their upraised lances.

Father waited for the whole column to

march by before he mounted his impatient steed and rode away. Watching him, Roger waved until every last Crusader disappeared over the edge of the hill. That was the last time he ever saw his father. He was six then.

Now the tall, round tower loomed in front of him. Blacker than the night, it was an eerie shadow that pushed Roger's doubts toward dread. Was his father alive or dead? Was Uncle Raimond real? With one arm across the curved body of the lute, he settled on the ground to wait for the night to pass.

IV. The Tower

Sun on his face woke him. He'd slept longer than he'd meant to. While he rubbed his eyes he looked around for his sister, but she was gone.

"Alice!" he shouted.

"I'm in here," she answered. "Inside the tower. Come see it."

Roger stood up to look at the tower from the outside. In daylight it seemed ancient. Its rough, weathered stones were furry with moss, and the peak of its cone-shaped roof had fallen in. *What could it have been used for,* he wondered. *A prison? A place to wor-*

ship moldy old gods? A defense against barbarians?

"Come on!" Alice called.

He picked his way over the remains of a wooden gate. Once it must have guarded the doorway to the tower, but it now lay rotting. Inside, he looked for his sister.

"I like it here." Alice's voice drifted down from above.

"What are you doing up there?"

A spiral stairway stood open and unprotected against the wall. If ever it had been enclosed in a shaft, the wood was long gone, but the stone staircase remained. The top step ended forty feet above ground.

Centuries before, the staircase had led to a floor that held archers, who'd shot arrows through narrow slits in the walls. Now only two thin boards remained between the top step and the wall, and Alice stood upon them.

"Come down this minute!" Roger yelled, his heart hammering.

"I won't fall," she told him. "I'm holding on to the window ledge. I can see really far from here, farther than from our sycamore tree at home."

"Get down!" he called, trying to mask the fear in his voice. "Those boards might cave in under you!"

"Oh, all right!" With nothing to steady her, because there was no railing, Alice skimmed down the stairs. Around and around, down and down—Roger squeezed his eyes shut.

When she reached him, she said, "You didn't give me a chance to tell you. From up there I could see someone coming through the forest."

"Who?"

"Two people, I think. Maybe they'll let you sing for our breakfast. I'll run and ask them."

Caution made Roger throw out his arm before Alice could reach the open doorway. "Wait! Let's see what they look like first. Stay here and keep quiet."

They heard branches crack, then men laughing and joking. "They sound jolly," Alice whispered. She and Roger peered through the opening where the tower gate had once stood.

Two men walked into what had been the courtyard. Each carried a dead quail by the neck.

"We could get strung up for stealing game, Simon," said one, a limping, filthy man.

"We've done lots worse things they could hang us for, Odo," answered the other. He was a thin, bony fellow whose bottom teeth were missing. "Stealing game's the least of it," he lisped.

"Right you are, Simon. Haw!"

"Anyway, nobody bothers with this part of the forest," Simon declared. "They've forgotten these old ruins. What a life we could live here, Odo! Undisturbed, like. There's plenty of game in the woods. Give us a couple of servants to wait on us hand and foot, and we'd live like kings."

"What's this?" exclaimed Odo as he caught sight of the lute.

"Don't know, but we can break it up for firewood." Simon raised the lute by its neck to smash it against a rock.

"*No!* Don't break it! It's mine!" Roger yelled. He dashed from the tower and grabbed the lute from Simon, who toppled to the ground in surprise. Before Roger could run away, Odo's arm flashed around his neck, and Odo's dagger pricked his throat.

"Leave my brother alone!" Alice screamed, hurling herself at them.

"By my whiskers, another one!" Simon exclaimed. He caught her in his long, skinny arms and held her straight out in front of him. Her feet flailed the air helplessly.

"This is the first time my prayers have been answered so swift," said Simon. The words whistled through his missing teeth. " 'Give us a couple of servants,' I said, and here they be! A fine pair of ragamuffins. All shabby and dirty, so they can't belong to anyone."

"We belong to ourselves!" Roger shouted. "Let us go!"

"We'll set you both down, but don't try and run," Odo said. "You're ours now. I always wanted a pair of servants."

"By my toenails, won't it be fun to give orders for a change, 'stead of always taking them!" cried Simon. "Boy! Hunt up some firewood. Girl! Pluck the feathers off those quail. Then cook them." Simon winked. "That's the way to treat servants, eh, Odo?"

"Right you are, Simon. Haw!"

Surely the men wouldn't keep them as they were threatening to! As long as Odo waved that dagger, though, Roger didn't intend to argue. While Alice plucked the birds, he gathered firewood, watching for a chance to speak to his sister.

"Bring your flint and help me start the fire," Odo called to Simon. The two men busied themselves striking the blade of the dagger with the flint, and Roger moved closer to Alice.

"Let's run," she whispered.

"They'd catch us. The lute will slow me."

He didn't want to leave it, not yet. Not until he decided how much actual danger they were in. "Wait a while. We'll see what happens."

After the fire was lit Odo said, "Servant girl, turn those birds on the spit. Nice and slow, so they won't burn." He scratched his raggedy clothes as though he had fleas, and turned to Roger. "Servant boy, while the birds cook, you strum us a song with that tune-twanger of yours. A gallant song for the likes of us, eh, Simon?"

"Right you are, Odo. One about fine, noble fellows, such as you and me."

"Haw!" laughed Odo.

Roger tried to remember a song about gallantry. Most of the verses his mother had taught him were love songs. Then he thought of the one she'd sung on the day they left home:

> *"My brother is a noble knight,*
> *An eagle guards his shield of white,*
> *My brother won't forgive a wrong,*
> *His sword is steel, his arm is strong."*

Simon's jaw, with its missing teeth, dropped open. "Where did you learn that?" he demanded.

"From my mother."

"Your mother! Who is your mother?"

"She's just my mother. My father's wife. My father is a Crusader."

"The Crusades have been over for a long time," Odo said.

Simon stared hard at Roger. Then, in a strange, slow, crablike motion, he circled the fire, never taking his eyes from Roger's face. Closer and closer he came, staring all the while.

Roger scrambled backward, holding the lute, but Simon kept coming. Suddenly the man pounced. "Got you!" he cried. "Grab the girl, Odo!"

When Alice tried to run, Odo caught her ankles and tripped her.

"O-ho, Odo, my friend," crowed Simon. "We're going to live like kings after all. I've just figured out who these two are."

V. Lady Blanche

"That ought to do it!"

The two men leaned one more log against the old gate. They had fitted it into the doorway and piled logs and rocks and brush and everything within reach against it, so it couldn't be budged. The tower was sealed.

"Now, Simon, tell me why we've locked up those two," Odo demanded. From inside, Roger and Alice could hear everything that was said.

"Ay, I will," replied Simon. "Until a few years ago, I served a baron whose name was Lord Raimond. I might still be serving him today, but he threw me out. Why? Because I stole one of his silver plates. Imagine! And him having so many."

Inside the tower Alice whispered, "Lord Raimond! Did you hear him, Roger? He said Raimond!"

"Shhhh! I don't want to miss anything!" Roger lifted a finger to his lips.

Simon added, "The baron had a sister called Lady Blanche. And that's who those two are, in there. Her children."

Alice clutched her brother's hand.

Outside, Odo scoffed, "Those two raga-muffins? If they're the children of a noble-woman, I'm Richard the Lion-Hearted."

"Then you must be King Richard," Simon answered. "Because by my eyelids I'll take an oath that those two are Lady Blanche's fledglings. 'Twas the song that tipped me off. She used to sing that very same verse to her brother, Lord Raimond. I remember the melody and her voice and the words. Even the lute looks familiar. I daresay she was playing that very one."

Roger and Alice stared at each other. Blanche was their mother's name.

"And when I took a good look at that boy," Simon went on, "I saw Lady Blanche beneath the dirt on his face. The yellow hair. The blue eyes. The same broad forehead. He's her image, he is."

Roger dropped his head into his hands. It was true that he and his mother looked exactly alike. But if she was a noblewoman, why had they lived like poor serfs in a tiny cottage?

"What are they doing here in the woods, then?" asked Odo.

"Who can tell? The last I heard of Lady Blanche, she ran away. Seems the baron wanted her to marry a rich old count, and she wouldn't do it."

"So she ran off?"

"With a penniless young knight from a family of no importance. The baron was furious. He searched everywhere for her. Then, when the knight was killed at the battle of Acre, he searched again."

Roger's eyes closed. It was certain, then. Father was dead. Everyone knew it—even these strangers. He clasped his legs and squeezed his forehead against his knees as though pressure could push away the grief, but tears seeped through his eyelids anyway.

Simon went on. "Lord Raimond never found Lady Blanche. She vanished, like. But now . . . *now* . . . !" His voice rose with excitement. "We've discovered her two brats. They'll lead us to her!"

"Right you are, Simon. Haw!" Then Odo sounded puzzled. "But what will we do when we find her?"

"Ask for ransom! He'll pay for the brats!

And he'll pay double for his sister! Our fortune is made!"

Odo burst forth with another "haw!" Then he added, "You're a fine, smart fellow to think of this, Simon. We'll guard them well."

"By my knees, we will! And we'll take our time to think up a foolproof ransom plan. Weeks, if need be. Those two inside will keep."

Weeks! Roger's heart sank even further. *Mother is so sick.* . . . Alice had the same thought. Her lips shaped the word *escape.* Roger nodded.

As the hours of the day ran out, they huddled together inside the stone walls, devising their own plan. When Odo passed roast quail and a waterskin through a hole in the barricaded door, Roger gave Alice his share.

At last the moon centered itself above the tower where the roof's peak had fallen through. A shaft of moonlight shone straight down on them, just as they needed it to.

"You don't have to climb up with me," Alice said softly.

"Yes, I do. I shouldn't be letting you do it

at all. I'm older than you. I should be the one to go."

"But you're too big," said Alice. "You can't fit through the space. I can."

Roger shuddered. In the pale light the window slit looked very high, and what Alice had to do seemed much too dangerous. He no longer had a father. His mother might die. How could he send his sister down that sheer stone wall in the dark?

Alice hugged him. "I'm glad you're going up the steps with me."

"I'll throw your shoes down to you once you're on the ground," said Roger. He winced inwardly as he pictured his sister inching down the wall in her bare feet. "After you find the lute. You'll make less noise if you search barefoot," he added.

Roger looked at the worn, slippery stairs of the spiral staircase he'd promised to climb. His stomach clenched like a fist. It was Alice, though, who would need real courage to slip through the window slit, climb down the wall, and hunt for the lute in the dark, without waking Simon and Odo. Then she had to find the road, reach Bordeaux, and search for their uncle. Roger groaned. He felt helpless. All because the window slit was too narrow for him.

"I hear them snoring," Alice said. "It's time to go."

Alice walked up the spiral staircase. Roger crept up after her on his hands and knees, clutching the edges of each stone step. She reached the top long before he did.

"Hold my shoes," she whispered when he got there.

Roger forced himself to stand on the rotting floorboards and take her shoes. Alice pulled herself onto the window ledge. Feet first, she eased through the narrow opening.

He held her hand until she got a toehold, watching her dig her fingers and bare toes into the cracks between the stones. He could see only the top of her head as she slowly worked her way down. *La Guenuche,* he thought, *braver than any* real *monkey.*

At last Alice reached the ground and went off in search of the lute. After many minutes she came back empty-handed, looking worried.

So she couldn't find it. They hadn't counted

on that. Roger knew that the lute, with its eagle carving, was proof of who they were. He shook his head and shrugged at Alice. Somehow she would have to manage without it.

He held out one of her shoes and let it go. She caught it. When he dropped the second shoe, she fumbled for a moment, but caught it too. Roger waved and Alice melted into the dark forest.

The moon had drifted past the torn roof when he turned to go back down the steps. The tower stood in total darkness. Roger gasped. He couldn't even see the stairway.

Terror made him clutch the window ledge. No matter how tightly he held it, he knew he was going to fall into the emptiness below. The two old boards beneath his feet would collapse, hurling him down. The thought made his hands slippery with sweat. He pressed hard against the wall, wanting to fuse himself to the cold stone.

"The stairs are solid," he whispered to himself. "I can do it. Alice climbed down a whole wall!" But his fear grew larger until it filled his skin and shook his bones.

He had to get down those stairs to begin the final part of the plan. Leaning hard against each step, he backed down like a baby. First one knee, then the other. Down, down. Take a breath. Beneath him, there always seemed to be another step. Why wouldn't they end!

Finally Roger felt the bottom. As he lay panting on the ground among the rubble, thankful to be alive, he thought of Alice, out in the forest somewhere. She was the brave one, and she was counting on him. Simon and Odo must not discover that she was gone.

Loudly, to fool them in case they'd awakened, Roger said, "You'd better go to sleep now, sister. Good night, Alice."

In Alice's voice he answered, "Good night, Roger."

VI. Lord Raimond, the Baron

"I'm the baron's niece," Alice said.

In the courtyard, laughter spread from one servant to the next—from men mending harnesses or polishing armor, to women brushing mud from boots and cloak hems, to children piling firewood against the wall. "Lord Raimond's niece!" Some chuckled. Others dropped their work to circle Alice, mocking her and making faces.

"What's causing this disturbance?" cried the steward as he came into the courtyard.

"This girl . . ." someone began, but Alice spoke up for herself.

"I'm here to see Lord Raimond, the baron. I'm his niece."

"Throw the scalawag into the moat," scoffed the steward. "The baron's niece, indeed!"

They reached for Alice but she skittered between them and ran. She hadn't traveled all this way just to be thrown into a moat!

For nearly two days Alice had searched for the baron's chateau, asking directions of everyone she met. A dozen times she'd lost her way. And she'd been hungry.

Once she'd rescued a cat from a tree, and its owner had rewarded her with a handful of plums. A baker had given her a bun for carrying a basket of eggs from the market to his shop. A housewife had poured her a cup of fresh milk, for no reason other than kindness.

But much of the time she'd been famished and footsore and shivery from worry. And now—"Catch the little baggage!" the steward shrieked as the servants chased Alice around and around the courtyard.

In one wall stood a wooden door decorated with iron bands. Alice threw herself against it and the door burst open into a great hall hung with beautiful tapestries and banners.

"What is this?" A very tall nobleman, with straight blond hair and a narrow beard, rose angrily from his chair. "Steward!"

"Forgive me, Lord Raimond," the red-faced steward apologized. "This child . . . she says she's related to you."

A young knight eating at the baron's table burst into laughter, but Lord Raimond was not amused. "Remove her at once," he ordered coldly.

The steward and the servants began the chase again, but Alice, too quick for them, scrambled up a rough stone wall. A little higher than their upstretched arms, she clung to a timber that supported one of the ceiling arches. "Listen to me!" she shouted down. "I am the daughter of Lady Blanche!"

The echo of her voice fell into a deathly silent hall. For years no one had mentioned Lady Blanche in Lord Raimond's presence. The only sounds were the sniffing of hunting dogs who searched for bits of food among the reeds strewn on the floor and the shuffle of servants' feet as they stole away. None but the steward and the young knight were brave enough to remain.

Lord Raimond's voice no longer sounded cold. Now it was hot with fury. "If you don't come down at once," he shouted, "I will order my archers to shoot you down!"

"You're supposed to be my uncle," she shouted back, "and you won't even listen to me! Mother told me to show you the eagle on the lute, but Simon and Odo hid it somewhere. And Roger can't get out of the tower, and Mother wants you to forgive her . . ." Suddenly it was too much for Alice, and she started to cry.

"Stop!" Lord Raimond raised his hand. "What's this about a lute? Come down here and make sense."

Alice lowered herself to the floor, but stood warily with her back against the wall. First she told Lord Raimond about her mother's illness. When he remained silent, she went on to describe everything else—the journey, Simon and Odo, and Roger's imprisonment in the tower.

"She claims to be your niece, my lord," remarked the steward, "but she looks nothing at all like you."

"That's true." Lord Raimond frowned. "If you're lying, child, it's a terrible lie for you to tell."

"Have you any proof?" asked the young knight.

"The lute was supposed to be proof. It's Mother's lute, but Roger can play it too. But it's gone."

The stern look had faded from the baron's face. "Come here," he said. "I will not harm you." When she approached he caught hold of her and drew her closer until she stood right in front of him. For a moment he stared at her, with eyes of the same blue as Roger's.

"The song your brother sang when the man called Simon recognized him," said Lord Raimond. "Can you remember it?"

"I think so. It goes: 'My brother is a noble knight, an . . .' " Alice's voice faltered. Then she caught sight of a blue eagle on a white banner behind the baron's chair. "That's the eagle on the lute," she said in wonder. "Not perched, but soaring, with an arrow in its beak."

Abruptly Lord Raimond turned to the steward. "Call half a dozen men-at-arms to saddle their horses," he ordered. "We'll set out for the forest at once."

"Does that mean you believe this urchin, my lord?" asked the young knight.

"I'm not certain. But nothing will be lost if we look for the tower."

VII. The Lute

No one, horse or rider, seemed to know which direction to take. Sitting in front of her uncle on his tall gray palfrey, Alice was as lost as the knights.

"Perhaps we're close enough to the tower that if we call out, your brother will hear us and shout an answer," the baron suggested. "Then we can follow his voice."

"No!" She shook her head. "Simon and Odo would hear too. They'd take Roger and run away."

The forest stood thick around them. To save time, the knights had bypassed the road to ride straight through the woods, but now no one knew which way to go.

"Can you whistle a nightingale's song?" Alice asked Lord Raimond. "I can't. Roger tried to teach me, but my whistle is too windy."

Lord Raimond smiled. "When I was a lad, I was better than anyone at bird calls."

"Then do a nightingale, please," Alice urged him. "Nice and loud."

After he did as she asked, another nightingale answered faintly in the distance, twice more.

"That's Roger," Alice said with a sigh of relief. "He'll go on whistling like that till we get there."

"Ride in single file and keep the horses quiet," the baron warned his men. "We want to take the outlaws by surprise."

They needn't have worried. When they rode into the clearing, Simon and Odo lay slumped against the tower wall, fast asleep. The remains of a roast pheasant lay between them.

Alice slid down from the baron's horse and ran to shake them awake. "Where did you hide our lute?" she demanded.

With snorts and splutters, the two ruffi-
ans rose to their knees. "How'd she get loose?"
asked Odo, still fuddled from sleep. "She's in
the tower! Each day I've heard her talking
to the boy."

Inside the tower Roger called loudly, "Is
that you, Alice? Make them let me out of
here!"

When Simon saw the baron's men around

him, he leaped to his feet. "That's my son you hear, my lords!" he cried. "By my nose, the boy's been such a scoundrel lately that I locked him up, for punishment, like. Keep quiet in there, son!"

"Suppose you set the boy free." The instant Lord Raimond commanded it, his men lowered their long lances to point at Simon and Odo.

Gibbering with fear, the culprits fell over each other in their haste to pull away the brush that blocked the door. As soon as Roger bounded out, Alice hugged him. Then she begged, "Help me find the lute, Roger! If we show it to our uncle, he'll have to believe us. The eagle on our lute matches the one on his banner."

Roger could not help staring at the knights. They seemed to spring right out of his memory. Though none of them wore armor—only metal helmets and leather breastplates—they loomed large and bold, like the men Father had ridden with. Their horses pawed and snorted impatiently, just as those long-ago battle horses still did in the shadow images of Roger's mind.

Which was his uncle? He wanted to ask Alice, but she was off looking for the lute. He searched the knights' faces for a sign.

"I see it!" Alice exclaimed. "It's up in that tree. No wonder I couldn't find it before! They've hidden it high in that oak."

Suddenly he knew with absolute certainty. His uncle was the tall, stern man who sat quietly astride his horse, studying Roger.

Straight blond hair showed beneath the rim of the man's helmet. A narrow mustache and beard circled his firm mouth.

"I'll climb the tree to get the lute," Alice said.

"No," Roger answered.

He'd mastered his fear of heights once before, when he came down the tower stairs in the dark. Now, with his uncle watching to learn what kind of boy he might be, he had to conquer the fear for good.

"You stay here," he told his sister. "I'll climb up and get it."

VIII. Ever After

Lord Raimond stayed at the door of the cottage as Alice and Roger ran to their mother's bed.

"You're back!" Zara exclaimed. "Your mother's fever is gone, but she still isn't—heaven's mercy!" The old woman clapped her hands when she caught sight of the figure filling the doorway. "You did bring him!"

Releasing Alice and Roger from her weak embrace, their mother raised herself on the bed. "Raimond?" she asked. "Is it you? I thought I dreamed it!"

With three quick strides he crossed the

room to kneel beside her. "I've come to take you home, Blanche," he told her. "To make you strong again." He took her hand gently. "I judged wrongly. Your husband was a good knight, a hero. I saw him fall at Acre trying to save his men."

"We waited for him to come back. We waited so long. . . ." She wept.

"Don't cry, Mother," said Roger. "Everything will be fine now. Uncle Raimond and I made plans while we rode here. We'll live in his chateau, where you'll get well. We'll take Zara with us too."

Old Zara threw up her hands. "Not I!" she exclaimed. "My old bones belong in my own cottage, with the sound of the stream outside to soothe me. Thank you just the same, but I'll stay here."

"I hate to leave, too, Zara," Alice said. Slowly she walked around the cottage, touching the rough table, the wooden bowls, the bench where she'd always slept beneath a soft sheepskin. "I won't enjoy having to dress like a lady all the time. I'll still want to climb trees and run."

Lord Raimond frowned at his niece. When

Lady Blanche saw the frown she spoke quietly. "Unless you're allowed to climb trees, Alice—and to marry whomever you choose—we'll all stay here. None of us will move to the chateau."

The baron turned abruptly to pace the small room. Then, with a slight bow toward Roger, he said, "There stands the next baron. Lord Roger. I have no children of my own, so I've made him my heir. Roger will decide what his sister can or cannot do."

"Alice?" Roger grinned when he looked at her. "She can do just about everything she tries. Since it's up to me, she won't have to marry anyone unless she wants to, and she can climb every tree for miles around the chateau."

Roger straightened himself to stand tall, no longer worried about his shabby, outgrown clothes. "I've already chosen the design for my banner," he told them. "On the right a nightingale will soar. And on the left . . . can you guess, Alice?"

"I hope it's a monkey."

"It is." Roger clasped her hand. "It will always be your banner as much as mine."

About the Author

GLORIA SKURZYNSKI is an award-winning children's book author. About *The Minstrel in the Tower* she says, "I've been interested in the Middle Ages since I was in my late teens. This period in history is so rich and exciting that I was fascinated by the idea of writing about it for younger readers. I hope they enjoy reading this story as much as I enjoyed writing it."

Gloria Skurzynski lives with her husband in Salt Lake City, Utah. They have five children and five grandchildren.

About the Illustrator

JULEK HELLER was born in Poland and studied painting at the Royal Academy of Art in London. He specializes in illustrating tales of fantasy and legend.

Julek Heller lives in London with his wife and two children.